To
JANE O'CONNOR:
This
is
yours,
all
yours.

PUFFIN BOOKS
Published by the Penguin Group
Penguin Putnam Books for Young Readers, 345 Hudson Street, New York, New York 10014, U.S.A.
Penguin Books Ltd, 27 Wrights Lane, London W8 5TZ, England
Penguin Books Australia Ltd, Ringwood, Victoria, Australia
Penguin Books Canada Ltd, 10 Alcorn Avenue, Toronto, Ontario, Canada M4V 3B2
Penguin Books (N.Z.) Ltd, 182-190 Wairau Road, Auckland 10, New Zealand

Penguin Books Ltd, Registered Offices: Harmondsworth, Middlesex, England

First published in the United States of America by Grosset & Dunlap,
a member of The Putnam & Grosset Group, 1997
Published by Puffin Books, a member of Penguin Putnam Books for Young Readers, 1999

1 3 5 7 9 10 8 6 4 2

Copyright © The Ruth Heller Trust, 1997
All rights reserved

THE LIBRARY OF CONGRESS HAS CATALOGED THE GROSSET & DUNLAP EDITION AS FOLLOWS:
Heller, Ruth, date
Mine, all mine : a book about pronouns / written and illustrated by Ruth Heller.   p.   cm.
Summary: Introduces various types of pronouns, explains how and when to use them,
and provides whimsical glimpses of what our language would be like without them.
1. English language—Pronoun—Juvenile literature. [1. English language—Pronoun.]
I. Title. PE1261.H394 1997 428.2—dc21 97-10051 CIP AC

This edition ISBN 0-698-11797-2
Printed in the United States of America
Set in New Century School Book

RUTH HELLER

WORLD OF LANGUAGE

MINE, ALL MINE

A Book About Pronouns

Written and illustrated by

RUTH HELLER

PUFFIN BOOKS

PRONOUNS take
the place of nouns...

so we don't have to say...

"Mike said
Mike walked
Mike's dogs
today.

Mike
walked
Mike's
dogs
a long,
long way."

How
boring...

what we say would be
without the PRONOUNS
his and **he**!

King Cole
would
call for
King Cole's
pipe.
King Cole
would
call for
King Cole's
bowl
and
King Cole's
fiddlers
three.

On and on...
it makes me yawn.
It's awkward and wordy.
The rhythm is gone.

And so...
hooray, hip hip hooray,
for
PERSONAL PRONOUNS
you, **it**, **them**, **they**,
for
us and **we**
and
I and **me**,
for
him and **her**
and
he and **she**.

These
are the most common
PRONOUNS
we use,
but
sometimes it's tricky
to know
which to choose.

Which should it be...the king
is
him
or
the king
is
he?

Reverse
the sentence
and
you'll see.

He
is the
king...
so
the king
is
he.

Are these for **he** and **I**, or are they for **him** and **me**?
Try each PRONOUN separately.
They aren't for I. They are for **me**.

They are for
him,
and not for
he...

so they're for **him** and **me**.

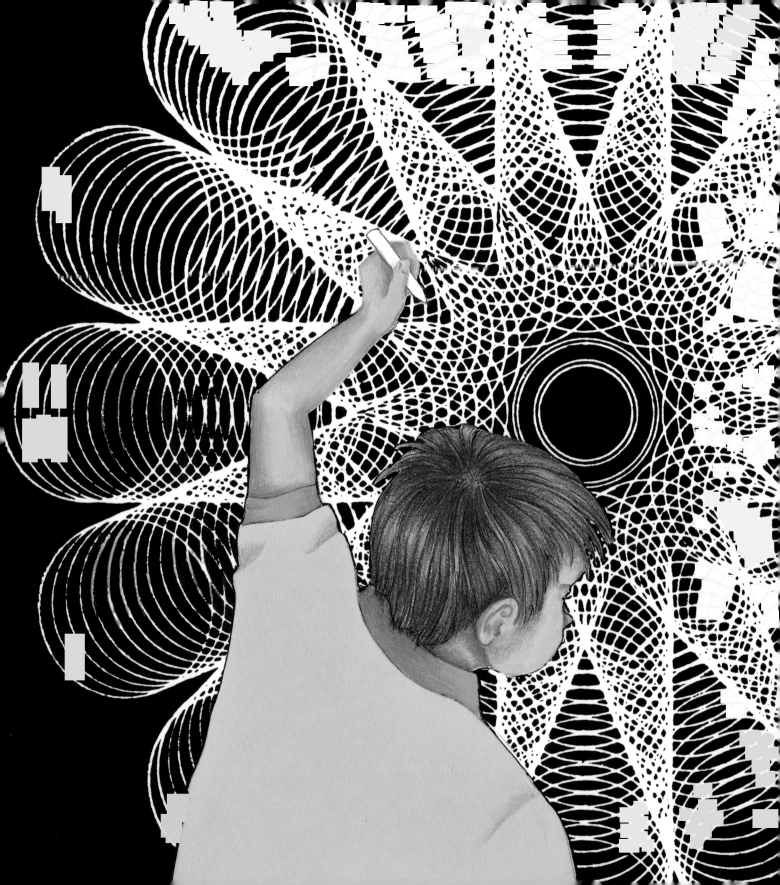

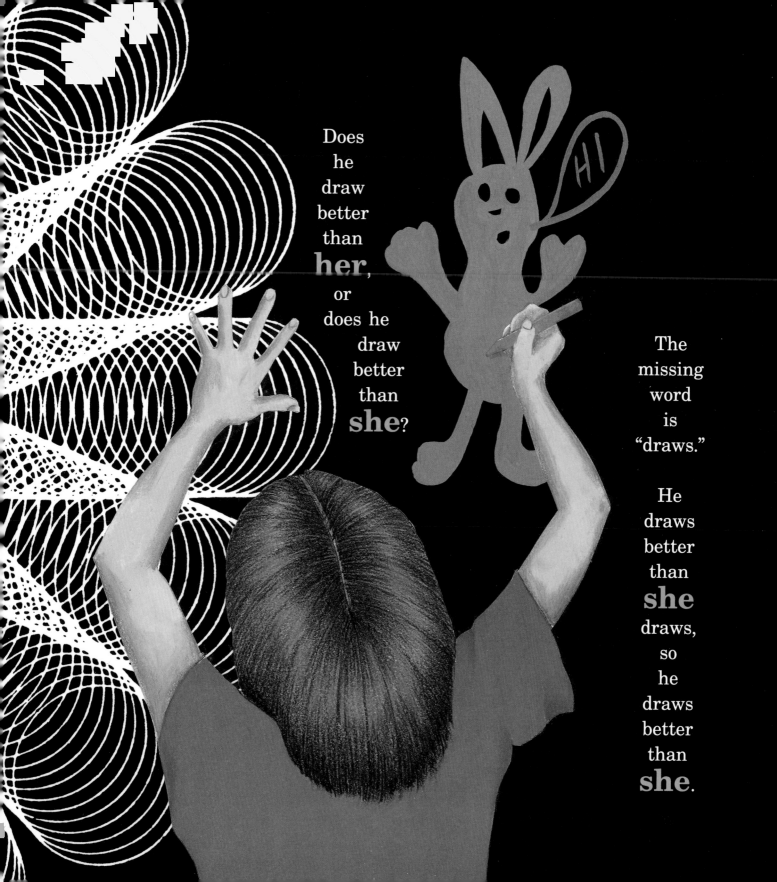

Does
he
draw
better
than
her,
or
does he
draw
better
than
she?

The
missing
word
is
"draws."

He
draws
better
than
she
draws,
so
he
draws
better
than
she.

We brag...so we (not us) Americans brag...

of fifty stars upon our flag.

But...
she
told
us,
so
she told
us boys,
that
we were
making
too much
noise.

Some PERSONAL PRONOUNS are also
POSSESSIVE.
All these presents are
impressive.

They are **mine**.
They are all
mine.
How
handsomely
their
ribbons
shine.

If...   I said,

"Everyone
stood
on **his** head,"
I'd be correct
but
not quite fair,
because
there are some
females
there.

His
or
her
head
is
what
I
really...

should
have
said.

DEMONSTRATIVE PRONOUNS make it clear.

Those
are
far.

These
are
near.

They
point out
decisively.

This is she, and that...

is he.

INDEFINITE
PRONOUNS
are
vague
instead.

Many
behind...

few
ahead.

Someone's
sleeping
in
my
bed.

REFLEXIVE PRONOUNS end in "self."
This messy elf just helped
himself.

REFLEXIVE PRONOUNS
are
INTENSIVE
when they emphasize or stress.

He **himself** made this mess. He made this mess **himself**
He is a messy elf.

The
elf
seems
more
offensive
with
the use
of the
INTENSIVE.

REFLEXIVE
plurals
end
in
"selves."

The
other elves
amused
themselves.

PRONOUNS
can ask
questions,
too.

INTERROGATIVE
PRONOUNS
do.

Who

had a nose
that
grew and grew?

RELATIVE PRONOUNS
make a
connection.

Here
is
Narcissus,
who
loved
his
reflection.

These three are all winners.

There's no way you can lose.

You
will
be
a
champion
whichever
one
you
choose.

Whichever's
a
RELATIVE
PRONOUN,
too.

When
should
you
say
whom,
and
when...

should you say
who?

Whom
is the one to
whom
something is done,
and
who
is the one
who
does it.

She is the one
who
was dressed in red
to
whom
the carnivorous
grandmother said,
"The better
to eat you
with,
my dear."

PRONOUNS
make our language flow.
These are
the
different kinds to know:

PERSONAL and POSSESSIVE

I me my mine
you your yours
he him his
she her hers
it its
we us our ours
they them their theirs

DEMONSTRATIVE

this that these those

RELATIVE

that which who whom whose
whoever whomever whatever whichever

INTERROGATIVE

what which who whom whose

INDEFINITE

all	everything	none
another	few	no one
any	fewer	nothing
anybody	fewest	one
anyone	little	other
anything	many	others
both	more	several
each	most	some
either	much	somebody
everybody	neither	someone
everyone	nobody	something

REFLEXIVE and INTENSIVE

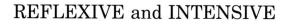

myself   yourself   himself   herself

oneself   itself

ourselves   yourselves   themselves

You will never
be
outclassed
if you put
"**I**"
or
"**me**"
last.

Say,
"he and **I**"
or
"him and **me**"
not
"me and him"
or
"I and he."

THE RUTH HELLER WORLD OF LANGUAGE

"To say that Heller has a way with words is to understate a multifaceted talent. . . . Rarely do books offer children so much to look at, listen, and learn."

—*School Library Journal*

A Cache of Jewels
And Other Collective Nouns

Kites Sail High
A Book about Verbs

Many Luscious Lollipops
A Book about Adjectives

Merry-Go-Round
A Book about Nouns

Up, Up and Away
A Book about Adverbs

Behind the Mask
A Book about Prepositions